THE HISTORY OF JAPAN IN A NUTSHELL:

From the Prehistoric Period to Modern Day

By Willowby H. Huxley

© Copyright Tonquin Publishing 2021 - All rights reserved.

The content of this book may not be reproduced, duplicated, or transmitted without direct written permission from the author or the publisher.

Under no circumstances will any blame or legal responsibility be held against the publisher, or author, for any damages, reparation, or monetary loss due to the information contained within this book. Either directly or indirectly. You are responsible for your own choices, actions, and results.

Legal Notice:

This book is copyright protected. This book is only for personal use. You cannot amend, distribute, sell, use, quote, or paraphrase any part, or the content within this book, without the consent of the author or publisher.

Disclaimer Notice:

Please note the information contained within this document is for educational and entertainment purposes only. All effort has been executed to present accurate, up-to-date, and reliable, complete information. No warranties of any kind are declared or implied. Readers acknowledge that the author is not engaging in the rendering of legal, financial, medical, or professional advice. The content within this book has been derived from various sources. Please consult a licensed professional before attempting any techniques outlined in this book.

By reading this document, the reader agrees that under no circumstances is the author responsible for any losses, direct or indirect, which are incurred due to the use of the information contained within this document, including, but not limited to, errors, omissions, or inaccuracies.

TABLE OF CONTENTS

Introduction 5

The Emergence of Japan 7

Feudal Japan 13

Early Modern Japan 19

Modern Japan 23

Fun Facts About Japan 31

References 49

INTRODUCTION

一期一会 – *"ONE LIFE, ONE ENCOUNTER."*

This Japanese saying originated from the Japanese tea ceremony 500 years ago. It was used to describe the importance of the present, suggesting everyone embrace this encounter as it may be the only one you have with your companion in your lifetime.

This saying sums up the essence of Japan and how the philosophy extends to every aspect of Japanese people's lives. Japan is a country with strict cultural traditions, yet it is also forward-thinking. Japan is a country full of history, and it has become one of the world's superpowers.

This book will dive into Japan's rich history and provide a brief insight into its most important timelines throughout history.

Chapter 1

The Emergence of Japan

Prehistoric and Ancient Japan

The Paleolithic period, lasting from 35,000 BC to 14,000 BC, displayed signs of the earliest human beings who lived on the Japanese Archipelago when the northwestern tip of Hokkaido was linked to the eastern extremities of Russia. They are thought to have learned skills that assisted them in making tools from stone. The prehistoric and ancient era continues with the Jomon period (from 14,000 BC to 300 BC) and the Yayoi period (from 300 BC to 250 AD) and covers the time up until the Kofun period (from 250 AD to 538 AD).

The Jomon era, which lasted from 14,000 BC to 300 BC, was one of the earliest periods in which Japanese culture emerged as one of the world's oldest cultures and is noted for its people's hunting and collecting traditions. They began carving pottery with a rope template style utilizing wet clay and produced jewelry from eggs, stones, bones, antlers, and other items, in addition to tool-making. The period was named after this cord style known as Jomon.

The Jomon existed for over 10,000 years until a more sophisticated race, the Yayoi, sailed across the narrow sea from the Korean peninsula around 500 BC. These newcomers eventually came to rule Japan, ranging from the Southern to Northern Honshu. It is now believed that the Japanese are descended from interbreeding between these two early inhabitants. While the people used to be hunters and gatherers, with the start of the Yayoi era (300 BC – 250 AD), they began to focus on paddy fields for rice production. Their society started thriving with the establishment of the first social class hierarchy. With these changes, areas of the world began to unite under the control of wealthy landowners. Unfortunately, we lack written records from this period in Japanese history. The only documents we have of Japan before the 8th century come from Chinese texts related to a country named *Wa* in the East.

During the Han and Wei Dynasties, Chinese travelers recorded that a shaman queen named Himiko (or Pimiku) reigned over Japan. We know that by 250 BC, a dominant regime had arisen during the Kofun period, operating from Yamato (modern-day Nara Prefecture) and controlling the land ranging from Northern Kyushu to Kinai. Kofun took its name from the large tombs built for the political leaders of that era, which also saw the arrival of Shintoism and the emergence of the Imperial House of Japan. Shinto (meaning "way of the gods") was gaining traction in Japanese faith, as the worshipping of various gods and spirits who live in nature (such as mountains, plants, and rocks, or express themselves in phenomena such as wind and thunder) was natural to the early cultures, where their very survival depended on the rice harvest.

The Beginning of an Empire

The Emperor settled in a constantly relocated capital from one region to another and ruled Yamato (modern-day Nara Prefecture). However, the Soga Clan quickly seized real political authority, culminating in a regime where most Emperors merely served as the state's emblem and conducted Shinto rituals. The role of the Emperor is believed to have arisen from the rank of the Shinto chief priest. According to legend, which can be found recorded in the Kojiki (or the "Record of Ancient Matters," which dates back to the early 8th century), Japan's first ruler, Emperor Jimmu, was the son of the Sun Goddess Amaterasu and was born in 711 BC. He ascended to the throne in 660 BC and died in 585 BC, making him 126 years old upon his death. As the celestial representative of the citizens of Japan, the Emperor provided authority to the ruling government — a guise that the politicians often abused. An assassination attempt on the Emperor, for example, would only expose the suspects to accusations of being unfit rulers of Japan, which would encourage opposing factions to seize power and influence. As a result, even as his strength waned, the Emperor was shielded by a mythological veil that no warlord, no matter how cruel, dared to pierce. Although the stories are not always accurate, it is widely believed that emperors reigned over Japan for over 1,500 years and are all derived from the same dynasty. A 16-petaled chrysanthemum flower serves as the imperial crest.

Classical Japan

The year 538 AD brings the beginning of the Asuka Period (538 AD - 710 AD), where Japan grew significantly from the mainland's good ties with the Kingdom of Kudara (or Paikche) on the Korean peninsula. Buddhism arrived from Korea in the middle of the 6th century, when Seong of Baekje, King of one of Korea's three kingdoms, sent a delegation to Nara bringing a Buddha statue and copies of the sutra. Buddhism was not embraced at first. The statue was cast into the sea after an epidemic destroyed the land, which was thought to have been brought by a tribal sun goddess who was angered that her citizens were praying to a foreign deity. The Soga clan's introduction of Buddhism and their eventual rise to dominance is regarded as the most important element in the spread of the religion in Japan.

Japan became known as 'The Land of the Rising Sun' under Prince Shotoku when he addressed the Chinese with the sentence, "From the sovereign land of the rising sun to the sovereign land of the setting sun." Prince Shotoku is reported to have played a particularly significant role in the spread of Chinese innovations. He also drafted the Constitution of Seventeen Articles, which outlined spiritual and political values. At the time, Confucianism and Taoism philosophies and the Chinese writing system had been applied to Japan.

Prince Shotoku was also connected with the Soga clan, who was pulling strings behind the ruling emperors. As time passed, the clan wasn't satisfied with being in the Emperor's shadow and started to display its influence and power by living in luxurious houses and building huge tombs for the family. Prince Shotoku's death led to the assassination of one of the heads of the clan, Soga no Iruka, which led to the elimination of the entire Soga clan, an event known as the Isshi Incident.

This Nara period displayed political changes influenced by Confucius' teachings, forming Japan's institutional and legal system, including criminal codes, official court ranks, and legal and governmental administration.

In 645 AD, we observe the beginning of the Fujiwara clan, which lasted until the rise of the Samurai and the Taika reforms. The Taika reforms was a new governmental and administrative system that followed the Chinese model, redistributing the land equally among the farmers while introducing a new tax system, first adopted from China. This system created many problems, resulting in decreased state income and internal political friction. The Fujiwara managed to control the political system for many centuries through intermarriages with the imperial family and enjoyed important political status within Kyoto and other major territories. Still, they started to decline when wealthy landowners hired the Samurai for their self-protection. This is how the Samurai became one of the most influential castes in Japan.

When the new Emperor, Go-Sanjo, decided to rule, the Fujiwara failed to control him, resulting in their end. The new government under the Emperor was called the Insei government and lasted from 1086 AD until 1156 AD when Taira Kiyomori became the new leader of Japan. We observe the appearance of aristocratic families such as the Taira and the Minamoto, which replaced the Fujiwara's people in important positions in the government and gained military experience.

The subjugation of the Northern Emishi people — descendants of the early Jomon who had largely existed outside the scope of control of the government throughout the South — brought further unification for Japan at the start of the Heian era (794 AD -1185 AD). The capital was moved from Nara to the Heian city (present-day Kyoto), where it would remain until 1868. The Heian period saw a proliferation in art and music, and history has bestowed a romantic label on it. During this period, the Tales of Genji, widely regarded as the world's first modern novel, was published, and the waka (a form of short Japanese poem) flourished. The Heian era is well remembered for the steady emergence of the Samurai class, an occurrence that would go on to dominate most of Japan's culture throughout the second millennium.

The concept of a central government in Kyoto led by the Emperor does not accurately depict the political landscape of the moment as strong warlords with their armies controlled the regions beyond Kyoto. After conscription ended in 792 AD, the Emperor was forced to depend on these clans to quell rebellions and maintain authority. His hold on control was tenuous, as he had to continually make sacrifices in exchange for their allegiance. Via the shoen system of land ownership, we can see the steady decline of central authority. With the advent of the ritsuryo in the mid-7th century, all lands were considered government property, and a tax was imposed to finance the administration. However, shoen lands were tax-free and given as gifts to all who vowed their loyalty to the Emperor. In this time, we see the appearance of the Samurai, who wealthy landowners hired for their protection.

As the balance of influence changed outward, the government became a more passive spectator of the conflicts outside Kyoto. In 1155, a succession conflict for the title of Emperor triggered a 40-year series of events that culminated in Minamoto no Yoritomo founding the Kamakura Bakufu —Japan's first shogunate — and obtaining the title of seii-taishogun (or "Shogun – Army Commander") in 1192.

CHAPTER 2
FEUDAL JAPAN

The Kamakura Era (1192 - 1333)

After crushing the Taira clan in the Gempei War in 1185, the Minamoto family seized possession of Japan. In 1192, Minamoto no Yoritomo created a new military government in Kamakura, the Kamakura Bakufu, and was named shogun.

Following Yoritomo's death in 1199, rivalries between the Kamakura Bakufu and the Imperial court in Kyoto erupted. Such rivalries for power came to an end in 1221 with the Jokyu disturbance, when Kamakura routed the imperial army in Kyoto, and the Hojo regents in Kamakura gained full control of Japan. They were able to win the allegiance of all the influential people in Japan by redistributing the land acquired after the Jokyu disruption. The Emperor and the remaining government offices in Kyoto effectively lost all influence.

During the Kamakura era, the Chinese presence remained reasonably powerful. New Buddhist sects were established: the Zen sect (founded in 1191), for example, attracted a significant number of adherents among the Samurai, who were now the ruling social class. Nichiren established another modern Buddhist religion, the militant and intolerant Lotus Sutra sect, in 1253.

The Joei Shikimoku, a civil document, was promulgated in 1232. It emphasized Confucian virtues such as the necessity of obedience to the master and, in general, sought to prevent a deterioration in morality and discipline. The Hojo clan retained a tight grip, and all traces of resistance were quickly extinguished.

The shogun remained in Kamakura without much influence, while his deputies were stationed in Kyoto and western Japan. Stewards and constables closely and loyally governed the provinces. The Hojo regents were able to get the nation several decades of stability and economic growth before a foreign force threatened Japan.

By 1259, the Mongols had invaded China and had developed an interest in Japan as well. Kamakura missed seeing many threatening communications from the influential Mongols. As a consequence, the first Mongol invasion attempt on the island of Kyushu occurred in 1274. However, after just a few hours of battle, the massive naval invasion fleet was forced to withdraw due to poor weather conditions. The Japanese were extremely lucky to have the assistance of Mother Nature as their chances of survival against the massive and modern Mongol army were not favorable.

Because of their careful planning, the Japanese mounted a solid defense for many weeks during a second invasion attempt in 1281. However, once again, the Mongols were compelled to retreat due to inclement weather. Kyushu stood on high alert for a potential third invasion attempt, but the Mongols quickly found themselves with too many issues on the mainland to think of Japan.

The long years of war preparations against the Mongols were disastrous for the Kamakura government because they culminated in vast expenses and no revenues. Many of the devoted soldiers who had fought for Kamakura were now hoping for compensation, which the government did not provide. As a result, financial woes and waning allegiance among influential lords were among the factors that led to the Kamakura government's demise.

By 1333, the Hojo regents' influence had diminished to the point that Emperor Go-Daigo could re-establish imperial power and overthrow the Kamakura Bakufu.

Muromachi Period (1333 - 1573)

In 1333, Emperor Go-Daigo was able to re-establish imperial authority in Kyoto and overthrow the Kamakura Bakufu. The resurrection of the old imperial offices under the Kemmu Restoration in 1334 did not last long because the old administrative structure was out of date, and inexperienced officials struggled to attract the patronage of wealthy landowners.

Ashikaga Takauji, who had previously fought for the Emperor, defied the imperial court and successfully took Kyoto in 1336. As a result, Go-Daigo fled to Yoshino in Kyoto's South, where he founded the Southern Court. In Kyoto, another Emperor was installed around the same period. This was made possible by a succession conflict between two lines of the imperial family that had raged since the death of Emperor Go-Saga in 1272.

Takauji became a shogun in 1338 and founded his government in Kyoto. The government and the historical era were named after the Muromachi region, where the government buildings were built beginning in 1378.

For more than 50 years, Japan had two colonial courts: the Southern and Northern courts. They had several fights with each other. The Northern Court was generally in a better position; nevertheless, the Southern Court was effective in taking Kyoto many times for brief periods, culminating in the regular devastation of the capital. The Southern Court eventually caved in 1392, and the nation restored its Emperor once more.

The Muromachi Bakufu governed the central provinces during the Shogun Ashikaga Yoshimitsu period (1368 - 1408) but eventually lost dominance over the outer regions. Yoshimitsu developed beneficial trade ties with

Ming China. Domestic productivity improved as a result of agricultural changes and the effects of a modern inheritance structure. These economic developments culminated in the growth of cities, various types of settlements, and different social divisions.

Between the 15th and 16th centuries, the Ashikaga shoguns' and Kyoto's government's power weakened to almost nothing. Members of land-owning military families became the Muromachi period's democratic newcomers (called Ji-Samurai). A few of them gained power over whole jurisdictions by first cooperating with and then surpassing regional constables. The new feudal lords were to be known as daimyo. They had significant influence over various areas of Japan and had been fighting against each other for many decades during the difficult period of civil wars (Sengoku Jidai). Takeda, Uesugi, Hojo in the East, Ouchi, Mori, and Hosokawa in the West, were among the most influential lords. Samurai were employing various weapons, including spears, bows and arrows, as well as guns, with the sword being their signature weapon. At the same time, they lived their lives according to The Bushido Code, otherwise called "The Way of the Warrior." The Bushido code included discipline, respect, and ethics and was influenced by Zen Buddhism. Wealthy landlords once again hired them for their protection.

At the same time, another class of warriors emerged: warriors specializing in unconventional tactics, creating constant chaos over the entire country. Their name is Ninja, otherwise "Shinobi", meaning 'those who act in stealth". Ninja used forgery and deceit to catch their enemies off guard, and they were not shown the same respect as the Samurai. The Ninjas' fighting method was called Ninjitsu and involved tactical strategies, geometry, meteorology, and breathing techniques. The fighting art was passed on to families or directly from masters to disciples. During the 15th and 16th centuries, several warlords employed the Ninja as mercenaries in castle capturing and fighting.

By the middle of the 16th century, some of the country's most influential warlords sought dominance. Oda Nobunaga was one of them. He took the first major steps toward Japanese unification by capturing Kyoto in 1568 and overthrowing the Muromachi Bakufu in 1573.

It is important to pause and try to understand the dynamics between the two powers, the Emperor and the ruling clan, as even with the internal frictions and the resurfacing of the Samurai class, the Emperor always kept his status as the supreme head of Japan.

Azuchi - Momoyama Period (1573 - 1603)

In 1559, Oda Nobunaga took possession of the province of Owari (which included the present city of Nagoya). He, like many other daimyos, desired to unite Japan. In 1568, he successfully captured the city due to its strategic location.

Nobunaga continued to destroy his rivals before settling in Kyoto. Among them were some radical Buddhist sects, especially the Ikko sect (or Pure Land sect), which had grown in power in several provinces. In 1571, Nobunaga dismantled the Enryakuji monastery near Kyoto. His conflict with the Ikko sect lasted until 1580.

Nobunaga was lucky in dealing with two of his most dangerous competitors in the East: Takeda Shingen and Uesugi Kenshin. Unfortunately, they both died before they could confront Nobunaga. After Shingen's assassination, Nobunaga used modern tactics to destroy the Takeda clan in the battle of Nagashino (1575).

General Akechi assassinated Nobunaga and seized his Azuchi castle in 1582. Toyotomi Hideyoshi, a general battling for Nobunaga, moved rapidly, defeating Akechi and seized power. Hideyoshi continued to destroy his remaining adversaries. In 1583, he conquered the northern provinces and Shikoku, and in 1587, he conquered Kyushu. Japan was eventually reunited after defeating the Hojo family in Odawara in 1590.

Hideyoshi burned numerous castles during the civil wars to gain complete control over the country. In the 'Sword Hunt' of 1588, he seized the arms of both farmers and religious establishments. He forbade the Samurai from farming and ordered them to live in castle towns. Hideyoshi felt that a strong differentiation between social groups could strengthen the government's grip over the population. In addition, a land survey was begun in 1583, and a census was conducted in 1590. Hideyoshi's massive fortress, Osaka Castle, was finished the same year.

Hideyoshi released an edict expelling Christian priests in 1587. Nonetheless, Franciscans were permitted to stay in 1593, and the Jesuits continued to operate in western Japan. Hideyoshi escalated his repression of Christian priests in 1597, forbidding more conversions and executing 26 Franciscans as a warning.

Following his dreams of world unification, Hideyoshi attempted to conquer China. In 1592, his troops conquered Korea and took Seoul in a matter of weeks; however, they were driven back the following year by Chinese and Korean forces. Hideyoshi refused to relent until the actual withdrawal from Korea in 1598, the same year he died. Tokugawa Leyasu, a wise associate of Hideyoshi and Nobunaga, succeeded Hideyoshi as Japan's most influential individual.

Chapter 3

Early Modern Japan

Edo, the Town, and the People's Time (1603 - 1868)

Japan's leadership was not the only thing that changed during this time. The country's capital was relocated from Kyoto, where the imperial court was housed, to Edo, now known as Tokyo. This is why 1603 marks the beginning of the Edo era, a time of peace and a society defined by the common people of Edo rather than by nobles. Much of Japan's well-known art, such as ukiyo-e wood printing, the kabuki theatre, and the kimono, was introduced during this period. A peaceful, secure nation meant advances in all kinds of technology, making many items far more available to commoners, including art and culture, which had previously been almost entirely the domain of the upper classes.

At the same time, Tokugawa Ieyasu became the most influential man in Japan, desiring to become the country's ultimate Emperor. The Samurai also became the highest-ranking social caste of the Edo period. They lived in castle towns, were the only ones permitted to own and bear weapons, and were compensated in rice by their daimyo or feudal lords. As a result, Tokugawa Ieyasu amassed almost limitless influence and riches. Shogun Ieyasu was named Emperor in 1603, founding the government of Edo. The

Tokugawa shoguns ruled Japan for an incredible 250 years, and during his reign, he cleverly redistributed the acquired land among his loyal subjects, expanding politically. Tokugawa Leyasu persisted in promoting international exchange by becoming allies with the English and the Dutch. At the same time, beginning in 1614, he enforced the suppression and abuse of Christianities.

After the Toyotomi clan was destroyed in 1615 when Leyasu seized Osaka Castle, he and his descendants had virtually no rivals left, and peace reigned in the Edo era. As a result, the Samurai were trained in martial arts and literature, philosophy, and the arts (including the tea ceremony). In 1639, traveling abroad was forbidden, and Japan was kept isolated from the rest of the world, except for trading with the Netherlands, Korea, and China. Western literature was also forbidden at the time. Despite the isolation, domestic trade and agriculture grew, especially during the Genroku era (1688-1703), where new art forms surfaced, such as the ukiyo-e and kabuki. Neo-Confucianism was Japan's biggest ideology at the time, which emphasized the role of morality, schooling, and hierarchical order in government and society. We can observe a four-class structure, with Samurai being at the top of the social caste, followed by the peasants, artisans, and merchants. The social status could not change, and outcasts or citizens of other occupations were part of a fifth class.

The prohibition on Western literature was lifted in 1720, and many modern teachings from China and Europe reached Japan. New nationalist schools emerged, combining Shinto and Confucianist components.

Even though the Tokugawa government stayed relatively stable for many decades, its status was slowly deteriorating for various reasons. First of all, the higher taxes were creating protests among the farming community. Also, Japan was plagued by natural disasters and years of drought, which increased the number of protests and slowly saw a rise of the merchant class, creating social chaos. Internal problems and low morale characterized this period.

When the Russians first attempted (but failed) to create trade relations with Japan at the end of the 18th century, external political pressure became an increasingly important problem for Japan. In the 19th century, they were joined by other European nations and the Americans when Commodore Matthew Perry finally persuaded the Tokugawa government to open a small range of ports dedicated to foreign trading in 1853 and 1854. However, commerce remained extremely restricted until the Meiji Restoration in 1868.

Chapter 4

Modern Japan

Meiji Period

At this time, we observe the rise of anti-government sentiments, which sparked other movements, such as calls for the Emperor's return and protesting against the West. This caused a civil war between the pro-imperial nationalists known as Ishin Shishi (who wanted to restore the Emperor to true control) and the shogunate forces (loyal to the military government headed by the shogun). In the end, the imperial powers triumphed. The shogunate surrendered in 1868, ushering in the Meiji Restoration, which restored the Emperor as Japan's sole monarch and permanently abolished the shogunate's military administration.

Furthermore, the Meiji period revealed the West's influence, with the Japanese wearing shirts, skirts and trousers, and following Western fashion standards in general. Modern industrialization was next.

The Tokugawa period came to an end in 1867-1868 with the Meiji Restoration. Emperor Meiji was transferred from Kyoto to Tokyo, which became the new capital, and his imperial rule was restored. The real political authority was passed from the Tokugawa Bakufu to a select party of nobles and ex-Samurai.

Like other subjugated Asian countries, the Japanese were compelled to agree to unfair deals with Western powers. These treaties provided Westerners with one-sided economical and legal privileges in Japan. Japan was eager to close the economic and military divide with the Western powers to restore freedom from the Europeans and Americans and develop herself as a respected nation in the world. In almost every region, drastic changes were implemented.

The new government's goal was to render Japan a democratic country with freedom for all people. Tokugawa Japan's social status distinctions were steadily eroded. In 1873, the amendments involved the creation of civil rights such as religious equality. The old feudal lords (daimyo) were forced to return all of their lands to the Emperor to stabilize the new regime. This was accomplished in 1870, and Japan was then divided into prefectures.

The school structure was reformed in response to the French and, eventually, the German systems. Most of these changes were the implementation of compulsory schooling. After one or two decades of intense Westernization, there was a resurgence of conservative and nationalistic feelings with Shinto and Confucianism values, like Emperor worship, being taught in educational institutions.

In an age of European and American exploitation, catching up in the military field was, of course, a top concern for Japan. Universal conscription was implemented, and a modern army was established modeled on the Prussian military and a navy modeled on the British one.

Many Japanese academics were sent overseas to learn Western science and languages to turn Tokugawa Japan's agrarian economy into an established industrial one. Huge government commitments were made to develop transit and communication networks. The government also directly aided the growth of companies and industries, especially large and powerful family businesses known as zaibatsu. The massive expenses caused a financial depression in the mid-1880s, accompanied by a currency reform and the founding of the Bank of Japan. The textile industry rapidly expanded and remained Japan's largest industry until World War II.

In terms of politics, Japan adopted its first European-style constitution in 1889. Although the Emperor retained control over the army, navy, executive, and legislative powers, a parliament, known as the Diet, was created. On the other hand, the governing clique retained real authority, and Emperor Meiji complied with the majority of their decisions. Due to a lack of cooperation between their founders, political parties were yet to achieve any real influence.

Conflicting positions in Korea contributed to the Sino-Japanese War in 1894-95. Japan conquered China and took over Taiwan but was compelled to return other territories to Russia, France, and Germany. The so-called Triple Intervention prompted the Japanese army and navy to ramp up their rearmament efforts.

New tensions in Korea and Manchuria between Russia and Japan triggered the Russo-Japanese War in 1904-05. Japan expanded its presence in Korea and annexed it entirely in 1910. The wartime victories by Japan increased independence even further.

Emperor Meiji died in 1912, and the reign of the clique of elder statesmen (genro) was coming to an end.

Taisho and Early Showa Periods: Ascension to Economic Power in Asia (1912 - 1989)

During Emperor Taisho's reign (1912-26), the political authority moved from the oligarchic clique (genro) to parliament and the democratic parties. Technologically, Japan was advancing so fast that it could compete with the Western countries. During World War I, the nation was a member of the Triple Entente, including France, the United Kingdom, and Russia, who all battled against Germany and Austria-Hungary. Japan was able to wrest control of territories in the Pacific from the defeated Germans, increasing its political and military strength. At the 1919 Paris Peace Conference, the United States, Britain, and Australia vetoed Japan's plan to add an 'ethnic balance provision' to the League of Nations covenant. Arrogance and ethnic hostility against the Japanese had troubled Japanese-Western ties since the country's forced opening in the 1800s. This became a significant factor in the breakdown of relations in the decades preceding World War II.

Japan's economic condition deteriorated after World War I. The Great Kanto Earthquake of 1923 and the worldwide slump of 1929 exacerbated the situation.

During the 1930s, the military gained almost total dominance over the country. Many conservative opponents were killed, and leftists were persecuted. Indoctrination and censorship of schools and the media were stepped up. Navy and army officers quickly filled the majority of key positions, including the prime minister's.

When Chinese Nationalists started seriously challenging Japan's position in Manchuria in 1931, the Kwantung Army (the Japanese armed forces in Manchuria) invaded the area. The next year, Manchukuo was proclaimed a sovereign state, with the Kwantung Army controlling it via a proxy government. The Japanese air force bombarded Shanghai the same year to shield Japanese civilians from anti-Japanese protests. Japan resigned from the League of Nations in 1933 after being harshly chastised over her conduct in China.

The Second Sino-Japanese War began in July 1937. A minor conflict quickly escalated into a fully-fledged war by the Kwantung army, which behaved somewhat separately from a more moderate administration. The Japanese forces successfully captured almost the entire Chinese coast and committed atrocities against the Chinese people, especially during the fall of Nanking.

As World War II broke out in 1939, Japan, along with Hitler's Germany and Mussolini's Italy, formed the Axis and invaded French Indochina (Vietnam) in 1940.

Pearl Harbor

In the summer of 1941, as retaliation for Japan's involvement in the French Indochina, the U.S. declared an embargo on aircraft exports and scrap metal and froze oil exports to Japan. At the same time, all commercial and financial relations with Japan ended. Japan relied on the U.S for 80% of its oil, and without it, its navy would not function. By destroying the U.S. Pacific Fleet, the Japanese navy would have a free passage in the Pacific. The Allied forces were weak in the Pacific. Japan launched a surprise attack on them at Pearl Harbor and many other locations in the Pacific, including Singapore, Hong Kong, Malaya, the Philippines, Guam, and Wake Island, in December 1941, giving them access to valuable natural resources including oil and rubber. Over the next few months, Japan captured major sections of Asia that extended to the borders of India in the West and New Guinea in the South.

Japan's loss at the Battle of Midway in June 1942 was a watershed moment in the Pacific War. From then on, the Allied powers gradually reclaimed Japan's captured territory. In 1944, intensive airstrikes over Japan began. In one of the bloodiest wars of the war, U.S. troops occupied Okinawa in 1945. In the same year, the U.S. dropped two atomic bombs on Hiroshima and Nagasaki on August 6 and 9, respectively, and Emperor Showa agreed to surrender.

After the War (Since 1945)

Japan was destroyed after the outbreak of World War II. Except for Kyoto, all of the major towns, factories, and transportation networks were heavily affected. For many years, there was also a serious food crisis.

The Allied powers' occupation of Japan began in August 1945 and concluded in April 1952. Its first Supreme Commander was General Douglas MacArthur. The United States was mostly in charge of the whole operation.

Japan effectively lost all territories gained since 1894. Furthermore, the Soviet Union held the Kurile Islands, while the United States governed the Ryukyu Islands, including Okinawa. Okinawa was restored to Japan in 1972, but a territorial dispute with Russia over the Kurile Islands has yet to be settled.

Japan's war machine was dismantled, and war crimes prosecutions were conducted. Hundreds of military officials attempted suicide just after Japan surrendered, and hundreds more were hanged for war crimes. Emperor Showa was not charged with war crimes.

In 1947, a new constitution went into force, and the Emperor was stripped of his civil and military authority, becoming nothing more than the state's emblem. Human rights were guaranteed, and universal suffrage was instituted. Japan was even banned from ever again leading a battle or maintaining an army. Shinto and the state were both distinctly divided.

MacArthur aimed to dismantle power structures by dissolving the zaibatsu and other major corporations and decentralizing the school and police systems. Concentrations of property holdings were eliminated as part of land redistribution.

During the first half of the occupation, Japan's media was subjected to strict suppression of all anti-American comments and sensitive issues such as ethnicity.

The collaboration between the Japanese and the Allies went reasonably smoothly. Critics began to rise as the United States behaved steadily in its self-interest after the Cold War, reintroducing communism repression, stationing more troops in Japan, and urging Japan to create its self-defense power against the constitution's anti-war provision. Conservative Japanese leaders welcomed certain facets of the occupation's so-called 'reverse path.'

The occupation concluded with the signing of the peace settlement in 1952. The Self-Defense Force of Japan was formed in 1954, followed by massive public demonstrations. The renewal of the U.S.-Japan Security Treaty of 1960 triggered widespread public outrage.

Japan underwent a major economic boom in the 1960s and 1970s. Economic development culminated in a rapid improvement in living conditions, social reforms, and the stabilization of the Liberal Democratic Party's (LDP) dominant status, making Japan one of the world's largest economies.

Japan's economic resurgence was demonstrated when it hosted the 1964 Tokyo Olympics. The economy continued to grow stronger, but in 1973 the oil crisis hit Japan, and the following two decades saw economic stagnation, accompanied by other historical events and natural disasters.

Despite economic stagnation, Japan remains a wealthy country today. It is also a country at the mercy of the elements. The earthquake and accompanying tsunami in 2011 killed over 20,000 and cost Japan billions of dollars.

From Crisis to Today

Every country envied Japan's growing economy in the 70s, as it was the first in gross national product per capita worldwide. In the early 90s, the bubble burst, and the economy stalled. The economic boom caused a stock market crash and a debt crisis for the banks and the borrowers, who couldn't meet their debts. The following years became known as Japan's "Lost Decade," a period during which economic growth froze. Japanese people were saving more and spending less, which maintained the problem. The effects of the economic crisis are still felt today.

Paying Our Respects

It is impressive to think how Japan was able to emerge from nothing to become a world superpower. Though we cannot conceive of the spirit and determination of the Japanese people, it's easy to see that they had to do a lot to become dominant players on the world stage. But, as much as various obstacles throughout history tried to keep Japan down, other catalysts promoted growth. A highly educated system with hard-working people in all hierarchies and the passion of the Japanese people, and their loyalty for their country helped them remain resilient through difficult times. Japan may not be the number 1 superpower globally, but no other country has shown itself more resilient to change than Japan.

Chapter 5

Fun Facts About Japan

Culture

There are different ways to be polite to one another, and every country has its etiquette – including Japan:

- ✓ In Japan, it is quite common to take off your shoes before entering someone's home.
- ✓ Tattoos may be accepted and even popularized in the West, but they can signify a criminal in Japan. Tattoos were widely connected with the Japanese mafia, known as the Yakuza; therefore, some places in Japan refuse access to people with tattoos.
- ✓ Eating with chopsticks is the norm in Japan, but passing on food using chopsticks is an insult.
- ✓ Tipping in Japan is not customary as it is in Western countries.
- ✓ Smoking is still permitted in closed spaces, but you will never find people smoking on the sidewalks or while driving.

Origin of the name "Japan"

Japan, or Nippon, means 'The Land of the Rising Sun.' The country was given this name as it was believed that Prince Shotoku addressed the Chinese with the sentence, "From the sovereign land of the rising sun to the sovereign land of the setting sun."

Flowers

Seasons and flowers are important in Japanese culture, as they represent the passing of time.

Japan is made up mostly of four major islands

Although Japan is an archipelago of about 6,852 islands, only Hokkaido, Shikoku, Honshu, and Kyushu make up 97% of Japan's overall landmass.

Japan has the second-highest life expectancy in the world

Japan has a life expectancy of 84.21 years old, making it the country with the second-highest life expectancy in the world after Hong Kong.

Tokyo is the world's most populous megacity

Tokyo metropolitan has an estimated 37.793 million inhabitants, making it the world's most populous megacity.

Forests cover 69% of Japan

When you think of Japan, you usually think of all the various cities that exist there. Surprisingly, forests cover the majority of Japan, accounting for 69% of the nation.

Japan has an unusually large number of active volcanoes

In Japan, there are a total of 110 active volcanoes. Scientists are actively monitoring and watching 47 of these active volcanoes, whether they have previously exploded or are at risk of an eruption.

There are over 1,500 earthquakes per year

Yes, you heard that correctly! Japan is one of the most seismically active countries globally due to its position on top of four separate tectonic plates: the Pacific, North American, Eurasian, and Filipino plates. Of course, most of these earthquakes are minor, insignificant earthquakes that you will not notice, but massive and destructive earthquakes occur on occasion.

The Kanto Earthquake of 1923 was the country's worst earthquake

The worst earthquake in Japanese history struck on September 1, 1923, with a magnitude of 7.9 on the Richter Scale. The earthquake is believed to have lasted 4-10 minutes, and almost 140,000 people were killed.

The 2011 Tohoku Earthquake, with a magnitude of 9.0 on the Richter Scale, was the deadliest earthquake ever to strike Japan, killing 29,000 civilians. Many people died in the fires triggered by the 1923 earthquake because many buildings were built of wood.

Japan is home to the world's deepest underwater post box

Guinness World Records set the mark for the deepest underwater post box in 2002 in Susami, a famous fishing town in Wakayama Prefecture. The post box is 30 feet underwater and has received tens of thousands of pieces of mail since it first came into existence.

Mount Fuji is a holy site

Mount Fuji is not only Japan's highest mountain; it has also been a holy site for the Shinto religion since at least the 7th century. Princess Konohana-sakuya is the Kami (divine person) of Mount Fuji in the Shinto Religion. The cherry blossom is her icon.

The Japanese have a strong attachment to nature

Most Japanese people have profound respect and love for nature due to the country's deep-running spirituality in the Shinto religion. This is due to Shinto adherents' belief that anything in existence, from rocks and mountains to rivers, is inhabited by spirits.

There are a lot of fish in the Sea of Japan

The Sea of Japan has a greater than average concentration of dissolved oxygen, allowing a wide variety of organisms to thrive in its waters. The Sea of Japan is home to over 3,500 animal organisms, including over 1,000 distinct types of fish.

Japan was completely isolated from the rest of the world for some time

Because of the tremendous impact that European culture had on Japan after their first contact in 1543, the Shogun of Japan, Tokugawa, closed Japan off to all outsiders in 1635. During this time, anyone caught using European items faced punishment. The Sakoku Edict of 1635 was the name given to this rule, which continued for over 200 years.

The world's last Emperor

Japan is the world's only nation with an emperor. Even if the Emperor of Japan has no influence and serves only as an emblem, they are also an important part of Japanese culture. The new Emperor of Japan is Naruhito, who ascended to the throne on May 1, 2019, after his father, Emperor Akihito, renounced the throne on April 30, 2019.

Japan has the world's third-largest economy

Since World War II, Japan has the world's third-largest economy.

There is a large number of hot springs in the country

Because of its geographical position and seismic activity, Japan has approximately 2,300 hot springs (called onsens) spread across the country. The water from these hot springs is said to cure various ailments, including rheumatism, arthritis, nausea, and chronic skin disorders such as eczema. The hot springs in Japan are said to have been found by ancient warriors and hunters. According to tradition, when these hunters followed the animals they had injured, they would always see the animals heading for these hot springs, which indicated the ability of the onsens to cure wounds.

The Shinano River is Japan's longest river

The Shinano River is Japan's longest river at 367 km and is situated on Honshu, Japan's main island.

Lake Biwa is Japan's largest lake

Lake Biwa is Japan's biggest lake, with a catchment area of 3,174 km^2.

Japan has one of the world's lowest unemployment rates

Japan has one of the lowest unemployment rates in the world at 2.9%.

Isewan Typhoon - Japan's most destructive typhoon

Each year, Japan is struck by typhoons, but the most destructive typhoon of 1969, the Isewan typhoon, killed over 5,000 people.

Great East Japan Earthquake – Japan's strongest earthquake

The Great East Japan Earthquake and tsunami were some of the strongest natural disasters in Japan's history. The Great East Japan Earthquake occurred on March 11, 2011, with a magnitude of 9.0 on the Richter Scale and was felt all over the country. The earthquake destroyed more than 122,000 buildings, and about 283,000 suffered severe damage, while approximately 748,000 more were partially damaged, with an approximate cumulative loss of $154 billion.

Kongo Gumi Co. Ltd - world's oldest company

Until being acquired and absorbed by the Takamatsu Construction Group in 2006, Kongo Gumi Co. Ltd, an Osaka-based construction firm specializing in constructing Buddhist temples, was the longest-operating company in the world. It existed for over 1,400 years.

It's hard to believe, but the business was established in 578 AD. It was involved in constructing some of the most prominent buildings in Osaka and Kyoto, including Osaka Castle and Hry-Ji in Nara.

Japan has the Shindo Scale for measuring earthquake intensity

Another fascinating aspect of earthquakes in Japan is how they are measured. While several areas of the world will report on the severity of an earthquake, Japan uses the Shindo Scale to determine its intensity.

Japan is the vending machine center of the world

Japan is the country with the most vending machines in the world, nearly exceeding 5 million machines.

Japan has just recently legalized gambling casinos

Throughout recent history, the Japanese could only gamble with pinball machines like Pachinko. Since gambling was illegal, they could only win metal balls, which could be exchanged for prizes or cash. Today, gambling casinos are legal in Japan.

Fake food is a trend

Japanese love fake food. Outside nearly any restaurant in Japan, you will find a fake version of the food served there.

Slurping noodles shows appreciation and compliments the chef

We in the West eat with our mouths closed as we believe it is more polite. But the Japanese believe that eating noisily is a sign of how much you are enjoying the food and therefore is a compliment to the chef.

Japan is one of the world's largest seafood consumers

Japanese people eat about 6% of the world's fish catch, making them one of the world's largest seafood buyers. China is the other nation with a high intake of seafood. This equates to approximately 28 kg of seafood eaten by each human per year.

In Japan, napping is encouraged

Napping at work is certainly appropriate in Japan as an indication that you have worked yourself to exhaustion.

Japan is one of the world's safest countries

Japan ranked #5 globally in the Safety and Security of the 2019 Global Peace Index, behind Iceland, Singapore, Norway, and Switzerland, and has been included in several foreign travel guides.

No shoes permitted inside

You would almost certainly be required to remove your shoes before entering any Japanese home and offered a clean pair of indoor slippers to wear. In Japan, as in other Asian nations, it is viewed as more hygienic to remove your shoes when entering someone's home. What distinguishes Japan is that this also occurs in restaurants and also in certain workplaces. Wearing shoes inside a house is considered impolite in Japan.

Japan has musical toilets

The musical toilets seen in Japan are one of the country's most distinctive features. These toilets steam the seat for you, wash you, and play music to block out any unwelcome noise.

Raw meat consumption is extremely common

Most people are aware of the Japanese preference for raw fish, especially in nigiri or sashimi. Many people don't know that Japanese restaurants also serve raw chicken sashimi (torisashi), raw deer sashimi (shikasashi), and raw horse sashimi.

In Japan, forget about the number 4

In Japan, the number 4 is considered unlucky since the sound is quite close to the word for death. In Japan, the number 4 is written as 'yon ()' or 'shi ().' Since the Japanese Kanji for death is 'shi (),' it is considered bad.

Nôgaku Theater – UNESCO intangible cultural heritage

Nôgaku Theater began in the 8th century when numerous Chinese performances were introduced to Japan. Nôgaku is composed of two styles of performance: lyric drama 'noh,' and comedic theater 'kygen.' Nôgaku is so common in Japan that it has had a significant impact on Kabuki and Japanese puppet theater.

Japanese specially grown fruit is considered a luxurious gift

Japan, apart from having weird square watermelons, takes fruit growing to an entirely different level. There are common fruits that can be purchased at a store for a fair price. There are also limited edition fruits that are handpicked and hand-grown, including, among others, the Aomori apple, berries, ruby roman grapes, yubari melons, and mandarin oranges.

Black cats are considered lucky and to be fortune tellers

Having a black cat can be deemed unfortunate in several nations, but not in Japan. A black cat crossing your path is considered a symbol of good fortune in Japanese culture. The Maneki-Neko figurine is one of the finest representations of black cats. While many Maneki-Neko are white, they are also available in black.

ASIMO – Japan's most popular robot

Japan is well known for its technological advancements, especially in robotics. The introduction of ASIMO (Advanced Step in Humanoid Ability) was one of the most well-known innovations. Honda developed this humanoid robot in the 2000s, and it was so famous that it played football with President Obama and danced for Chancellor Angela Merkel. This robot is on show at the Miraikan Museum in Tokyo, Japan.

Children learn how to clean from an early age

Japanese teachers work together with students to clean the classroom.

Sushi has been a popular dish since the 2nd century AD

Since the 2nd century, sushi has been a part of Japanese culture. It started as a method of preserving fish in China and gradually spread to Japan. Sushi entails consuming fish and rice with vinegar, salt, and sugar seasonings.

The world-renowned Kobe beef

Japanese Kobe beef is popular all over the world for its exceptional succulence and unrivaled flavor. What distinguishes the meat is the breed of cows from which it is derived and the level of treatment given to the livestock. It is claimed that they are fed beer to make them enjoy a happier and stress-free existence and that they are given massages to help with any cramps they might have. If you're worried about ordering or purchasing Kobe beef, bear one thing in mind: some people confuse Wagyu and Kobe.

Wagyu is a Japanese word that means 'Japanese cow.' All Kobe is Wagyu, but not all Wagyu is Kobe, and there are rather stringent grading requirements that must be followed for it to be Kobe beef.

Japan is the third-largest car manufacturer in the world

Japan is one of the world's leading automakers, behind only China and the United States in overall unit volume. Toyota, the Japanese automotive giant, is the world's largest automobile maker.

One of Japan's favorite sports is sumo wrestling, with a 1,500-year background

Sumo wrestling has been practiced in Japan for over 1,500 years. The wrestlers here weigh an average of 300 pounds and practice in Heya rooms supervised by former champions. Traditionally, the younger wrestlers are expected to clean and care for the veteran wrestlers. The most intriguing aspect of Sumo wrestling is that it is a Shinto rite intended to show respect and appreciation to the spirits. Sumo seems strange at first glance, as overweight men clad in gigantic thongs press each other within a narrow ring, and the pre-ceremony is normally longer than the actual battle. However, look a little closer. You will discover a fascinating and technical discipline with a rich past like Samurai, as well as wrestlers whose strict preparation routine and determination cannot fail to impress.

Sumo is believed to have originated from a Shinto ceremonial dance. The strongest men demonstrated their bravery in front of the kami (gods or spirits) as a show of praise and thanks for bringing in a successful harvest. Afterward, it was used to compare intensity to assess which warriors were the most skilled in hand-to-hand fighting. Professional sumo wrestlers did not rise from the ranks of amateurs until the Edo era when daily tournaments started. The best fighters started to achieve star status, and sumo's success soon spread among the general public.

In Japanese, sumo wrestlers are classified as rikishi (the two characters of the kanji that mean 'power' and 'warrior'). Sumo has different classes, with the top class attracting the most public exposure.

Sumo's pre-match ceremony is also exciting, as we can observe the offering to the gods of salt, rice, dried kelp, dried chestnuts, dried cuttlefish, and nutmeg. The sumo warriors enter the ring from the East and West, with the one warrior entering from the east side first. Both join the ring and execute a move known as shiko — the leg raising and stomping that is more widely connected with the sport outside of Japan. The clapping of hands draws the gods' attention; the lifting of arms to the heavens is to prove they have no weapons, and the famous leg raising and stomping are to crush any remaining evil spirits. When the shiko is completed, the fighters leave the circle to cleanse themselves. The first rite is known as chikara-mizu (literally 'power water'), and each fighter receives it from the last fighter they beat. Each fighter will take a scoop of water and swill it in their mouth, similar to the washing procedure at shrines and temples. Before joining, they take a pinch of kiyome-no-shio (cleansing salt) and throw it over the ring. When the referee (gyji) signals for the bout to begin, each fighter crouches behind a white line known as the shikirisen on their half of the ring. When all warriors have their clenched fists lying on or behind their shikirisen, the battle starts. Since the rikishi determine the start of the bout, the moments leading up to it may be very stressful for the fighters. The fighter often crouches for a few seconds, watching to see what their enemy does before rising to recompose themselves.

They can exit the ring to their respective corners; however, they must cleanse the ring with salt again before re-entering. One bout determines the victor, and since the first few seconds in which the rikishi clash always determine the champion, you can see that the pre-bout rituals are often the most exciting moments of the fight.

Japan has a rabbit island

Okunoshima Island is a tiny island in Hiroshima Prefecture that is filled with rabbits. During World War II, the island was a production center for toxic gases, which were sadly experimented with on rabbits. The rabbits escaped during World War II, and the offspring of these research rabbits are the ones you can see on the island today. It is believed that over 1,000 rabbits still live on the island.

The bowing etiquette

Bowing is considered the most common and culturally appropriate type of social etiquette in Japan. Bows are categorized into three types: traditional, formal, and casual. Although formal bows are produced at a shorter angle of 15 degrees, very formal bows entail bending at a 30-degree angle. The deepest bow denotes greater reverence.

Japan has the world's busiest train station

Shinjuku Station in Tokyo is the busiest train station in the country. It is used by almost 3.6 million individuals regularly, which is mind-boggling to consider. What is perhaps more astounding is the volume of train use in Japan as a whole. Only six of the world's top 51 busiest train stations are not in Japan.

The world's first novel was published in Japan

The Tale of Genji is widely regarded as one of the best works of Japanese literature and the world's first book. Murasaki Shikibu, a Japanese woman, published it. It is claimed that some of the emotional motivation for the book came from her husband's death, which had a significant influence on her.

The ringing of the bells

Every year on New Year's Eve in Japan, temple bells are rung 108 times to usher in the new year. Several temples in the area will begin ringing their bells before 11 p.m. and will ring them 107 times before midnight. They will then sound the bell one more time to usher in the new year.

Bugaku and gagaku: The world's oldest dance and music traditions

Bugaku is a popular dance held for Japanese elites in imperial courts, and gagaku is the accompanying song. This song is the world's oldest recorded court music and dance hybrid. Before World War II, this combination of dance and music was mainly used by the Japanese aristocracy. It was only after the war that it was made available to the general public.

Baseball is the most popular sport by far

Baseball was invented in 1873 by the American Horace Grant, and it has been the most common sport in Japan ever since. Currently, Japan has one of the most active professional baseball leagues globally, producing promising ballplayers who have done well in Major League Baseball, such as Ichiro Suzuki, Hideki Matsui, and Hideo Nomo.

Capsule hotels

Although initially developed for business travelers, capsule hotels have become popular among low-budget travelers and tourists.

Love hotels

Love hotels are small boutique hotels with rooms equipped with erotic programs and other erotic accessories.

Takotamago

Takotamago is one of the most delicious foods globally and very popular among tourists in Japan. It is the perfect snack and involves a small octopus served on a stick, with a cooked egg in its head.

Cute food

The Japanese were the first to start creating cute food. This means you will find a lot of food, ice cream, and other desserts in the shape of a dog, cat, frog, and any other cute shape you want.

Ainu

The Ainu (アイヌ), also known as Ezo in historical texts, are people indigenous to the lands of northern Japan, the original inhabitants of Hokkaido. The Ainu are believed to be descendants of the Jomon people, otherwise known as the Mongoloid migrants who entered the Japanese islands before the Jomon period. They were later gradually displaced and assimilated when the Yamato Japanese expanded their territory from western Japan northwards over the past 1,500 years. History shows that in the 18th century, there were 80,000 Ainu, which assimilated into the Japanese culture together with their land, language, religion, and customs. The Ainu were first employed in the military in 1898 during the Russo-Japanese War and later in the Second World War.

Thank you for purchasing a copy of this book. I certainly hope you learned something!

Want all of my future books for FREE before they are released to the public? Visit www.HistoryInANutshell.ca/Review-Team to learn more!

CHAPTER 5: REFERENCES

REFERENCES

A Teacher's Resource: Home: Japan Society. About Japan (n.d.) https://aboutjapan.japansociety.org/

Beasley, W. (1991-04-04). Japanese Imperialism 1894–1945: Oxford University Press. Retrieved May 10. 2021, from https://oxford.universitypressscholarship.com/view/10.1093/acprof:oso/9780198221685.001.0001/acprof-9780198221685

History.com (2009, October 29). *Pearl Harbor.* History.com https://www.history.com/topics/world-war-ii/pearl-harbor

"Japan: Memoirs of a Secret Empire" PBS, Public Broadcasting Service, www.pbs.org/empires/japan/index.html

www.ingramcontent.com/pod-product-compliance
Lightning Source LLC
Chambersburg PA
CBHW041310110526
44590CB00028B/4317